# THE VIKING SHIPS
# IN OSLO

BY

THORLEIF SJØVOLD

UNIVERSITETETS OLDSAKSAMLING

OSLO 1985

# CONTENTS

|  | Page |
|---|---|
| INTRODUCTION .. .. .. .. .. .. .. .. .. | 5— 9 |
| THE OSEBERG FIND .. .. .. .. .. .. .. .. | 10—52 |
|     I. Excavation and Preservation .. .. .. .. .. | 10—20 |
|     II. The Ship .. .. .. .. .. .. .. .. .. | 22—36 |
|     III. The Grave Furniture .. .. .. .. .. .. | 36—52 |
| THE GOKSTAD FIND .. .. .. .. .. .. .. | 53—68 |
| THE TUNE SHIP .. .. .. .. .. .. .. .. .. | 69—70 |
| THE BORRE FIND .. .. .. .. .. .. .. .. | 71—72 |
| CONCLUSION: The Significance of the Viking Ship Finds | 73—77 |
| BIBLIOGRAPHY .. .. .. .. .. .. .. .. .. | 78—79 |
| LIST OF ILLUSTRATIONS .. .. .. .. .. .. .. .. | 80 |

That the Vikings built and navigated ships has been common knowledge ever since the name *Viking* was first heard. In fact, without ships the great out-going activity which is so typical of the period known as the Viking Age would not have been possible. Moreover, the ships they used must have been good ships, strong and sufficiently sea-worthy to cross the North Sea even in a storm; but at the same time they had to be light enough to be hauled across long distances on land, when necessary. As time went on, such ships crossed the ocean to Iceland and Greenland, and from there the Norsemen sailed their ships to America, at least as far as Newfoundland.

The sagas are full of accounts of ships and sea-voyages, but they tell us little about the construction and appearance of these vessels. The people for whom they were composed did not need to be told what a Viking ship looked like; modern readers can visualize a car without having the internal combustion engine explained to them!

As long as our knowledge about Viking ships depended exclusively on literary sources, we therefore knew very little about the construction and building of these vessels. True, there were a few illustrations depicting such ships: a series of tomb stones on Gotland has incised pictures showing large and small Viking ships under sail, and the famous Bayeux tapestry illustrates William the Conqueror's navy on its way across the Channel to invade England. These illustrations do provide some information about the appearance of the ships and their spread of sail, but by no means enough to enable a modern shipwright to make a plausible copy of a Viking ship simply on the basis of these representations and the testimony of the sagas. And as long as this was out of the question, our knowledge about the Viking ships was sadly inadequate.

The discovery and excavation of the Tune ship in 1867 and the Gokstad ship in 1880 meant a tremendous advance in this field. Now we had an answer to practically all our questions regarding the construction and building of the Viking ships and about the way in which practical problems large and small were solved—and about these matters the sagas say almost nothing. And then, in 1904, the third and last of the "classic" Viking ship finds was uncovered— the Oseberg ship. Although this craft cannot compare technically with the Gokstad ship, which far surpasses it as a sea-going vessel, the wealth of the grave furniture accompanying this ship burial provides quite a unique illustration of important aspects of the cultural life of the Viking Age, not least of the creative powers of the artists of the time.

All these three ships may now be seen in the Viking Ship Hall at Bygdøy in Oslo, and we hope that this booklet may provide an answer to some of the questions likely to be asked by the visitor to this exhibition; that is its main purpose. The tour of the hall has its natural starting point in the Oseberg ship—this catches the visitor's eye on entering the building. Then one will turn to the Gokstad ship and the Tune ship, and the last part of the visit is likely to be spent on a study of the wealth of equipment and grave furniture found together with the Oseberg ship and the Gokstad ship; this material is on display in the fourth—and last—wing of the Viking Ship Hall. A small collection of objects from a ship find at Borre is also included in the exhibition. Our booklet starts with a description and discussion of the ships and other material from Oseberg and Gokstad, the main stress being laid on Oseberg, the richest find of them all. These chapters are followed by a discussion of the Tune ship, while the Borre find comes at the end.

For a long time our three Viking ships were to remain the only tangible reminiscences of the shipwright's craft in the Viking Age, but now this is far from being so. In the summer of 1962, considerable remains of five Viking ships were uncovered near Skuldelev in the Roskilde Fiord in Denmark. They had been sunk there in order to blockade a ships' channel which led in to Roskilde. Now these ships have been restored, and the museum in Roskilde where they are displayed in immediate contact with the fiord is devoted entirely

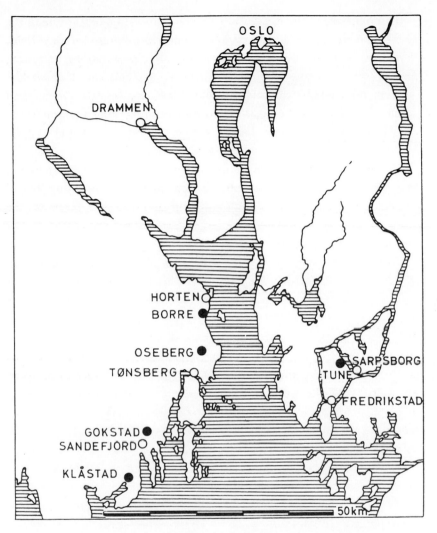

*Sketch map of the sites.*

to them.—And in 1970 yet another addition to the extant Viking ship fleet came to light: a partly preserved Viking ship was excavated on the land of the farm Klåstad at Tjølling, Vestfold. This ship has now been preserved, and restored as far as the available evidence permitted. Since 1977 it has been on display at the Vestfold County Museum in Tønsberg.

7

Thus in the course of a few years the number of known, more or less preserved ships from the Viking Age has increased threefold. It goes without saying that this has added considerably to our knowledge of ship-building as it was practised during the Viking Age, not least because the new finds not only give us a far wider geographical distribution, but also span a greater period of time. Considerably more types are now known, and far more variation in construction and ship-building technique than we had previously been aware of has been manifested. We have every reason for expecting more Viking ships to come to light, not least because of the greatly increased interest in ancient ships inspired by modern underwater archaeology.

But even so the number of preserved ships from the Viking Age is likely to remain extremely small as compared to the number of ships that must actually have been built and used in the North in the course of that period (c.A.D. 800—1030). The question naturally arises: why have precisely these nine ships come down to us? By way of an answer we must remember that the span of life of ships is brief if we apply archaeological concepts of time: only under unusually favourable conditions will a ship have a chance of remaining in a reasonable state of preservation for a thousand years or so.

The humid surroundings in which they lay is the main reason for the—at least partial—preservation of these nine ships: the Danish ships lay under water, and most of the Norwegian ships were buried in blue clay, which is found in the subsoil in the counties of Østfold and Vestfold. The Klåstad ship was probably wrecked and left lying on the shore until it was silted down. As the land has risen here since the Viking Age, this craft lay several hundred metres inland when it was found. The other three ships were all used as burial-ships: they were hauled ashore, and the dead were buried in a large burial chamber erected in or over the after-ship; finally a large barrow was raised to cover the entire burial. All this will be discussed at greater length in connection with each of the finds. —

The first edition of the present booklet was entitled "The Oseberg Ship and the other Viking Ship Finds". "The others" were, at the time of writing, the Gokstad ship and the Tune ship, that is all. Information deriving from more recently discovered finds was included in later editions as it became available. The text has undergone yet a further revision for the purpose of the present edition, a number of new illustrations are included, and the title has been changed, as the original title was no longer adequate. Now «the other» Viking ship finds comprise a considerably greater number than the original two, but as this booklet is first and foremost intended for visitors to the Viking Ship Hall at Bygdøy, we saw no reason for including a detailed discussion of ships not on display here.

# THE OSEBERG FIND

## I. EXCAVATION AND PRESERVATION

The excavation of the Oseberg find took place during the summer of 1904 on the Oseberg farm at Slagen, not far from Tønsberg. The archaeologist in charge of this work was Professor Gabriel Gustafson of the University of Oslo.

*The grave mound*  The ship and burial chamber had been covered by a very large grave mound, 44 metres in diameter and originally about 6 metres high; the subsoil had subsided, however, so that at the time when the excavations began, the mound was only about 2¹/₂ metres high. The local soil was clay, but the mound itself was built of an enormous number of turf sods, packed tightly together with the grass side up. The mound thus formed a fairly compact, air-tight cover over the ship and all its contents. This, together with the blue clay of the subsoil, has resulted in the remarkable preservation of all the wooden objects and other articles of organic material for more than a thousand years.

But the ship and its contents had not stood undisturbed in the barrow. At some time or other, probably in the early Middle Ages, robbers had broken into the grave mound, hewn a hole in the bow of the ship, and made their way to the burial chamber aft. The grave itself was thus seriously disturbed, and many of the contents were found in the entrance made by the robbers.

The ship was also in a sad state when it was excavated. At the time of the burial it had been filled with quantities of stones, and the weight of these as well as that of the actual mound with all the stones which had been piled up around the ship, had resulted in a considerable subsidence of the ground under the mound. The ship had thus been broken up into thousands of small fragments which had to be taken up one by one and later laboriously put together.

10

*From the excavation of the Oseberg ship: the stern exposed, seen from port side.*
*Photo Væring.*

Most of the rich furniture which had been buried with the dead was found in the fore-part of the ship. First there were a great number of ship's accessories here: oars, a gangway, a bailer, tubs and pails etc. Here, too, were a richly decorated cart, three beautiful sleighs and a working sled, as well as three finely carved sleigh shafts. Among the fine, carved work special mention must be made of one of the animal head posts. Three beds and two tents were included in the equipment and, finally, the skeletons of at least 10 horses.

The skeletons of some horses and an ox were also found just beside the ship, and a further skeleton of an ox astern, outside the burial chamber. A number of kitchen utensils were also found here. In the entrance made by the robbers lay the remains of human skeletons, which show that two women were buried on the ship; they doubtlessly lay in beds in the burial chamber, and the quantities of textile remnants, down and feathers must come from the bedding and the decorations in the chamber.

A number of the more personal possessions of the dead were also found in the burial chamber: implements for textile work, chests, buckets and four beautiful animal head posts. All of these were fitted with "shafts" and were discovered close to the peculiar "rattles".

It is remarkable that there were no traces of jewelry; personal jewelry was an integral part of the equipment for a Viking woman's grave. The total absence of jewelry in the richest grave that has been discovered cannot be due to coincidence, and it appears most likely that jewelry provided the incentive for the plundering of the grave.

If the excavation of the Oseberg find was an enormous and difficult task, that of restoring and preserving it proved to be no easier. First and foremost it was the *wooden articles* which gave rise to difficulties, partly because they were in a very poor condition, and partly because there was a lack of experience in this field. The museums had some knowledge of work with antique metal objects, but those in the Oseberg find presented no problems; even the objects made of iron are in quite remarkably good a condition.

12

*The Oseberg ship in the mound: the whole ship exposed and
the burial chamber and all the equipment removed. Photo Væring.*

The wooden objects were far more difficult, and the matter was still further complicated by the fact that these could not be considered as one entity: they were of different kinds of wood and were found in very different states of preservation. It was clear from the start that it would not be possible to use one method of preservation for them all. Three methods were used to begin with— one for the ship itself, another for the cart, the sleighs and most of the other large objects, and yet at third method for the smaller objects with particularly fine carving (the animal head posts and the sleigh shafts).

*The ship*
*The ship* itself was the largest "object" in the find, but all the same it gave rise to the fewest problems in the matter of treating it for preservation. Here the Tune and Gokstad ships had provided some experience, although neither of these had been damaged to the same extent.

Every one of the countless fragments into which the ship had been broken was carefully marked, numbered and then individually removed from the mound. The fragments were washed, impregnated with creosote and linseed oil, and temporarily stored in a shed erected for the purpose on the site of the excavation. They were later taken to Oslo where the work of restoration was to be done.

The individual fragments into which the ship had been broken had been greatly bent and deformed by the pressure of the mound. Piece by piece they had to be laboriously steamed and pressed into their original shape. Although this work took a long time, it made it possible to rebuild the ship almost completely with the original fragments; only the rivets are mostly new. The ship was finally protected by a coat of mat varnish.

The Oseberg ship was re-assembled in a temporary shed in the University grounds. It stood here for nearly twenty years before it could be moved, in 1926, to the new Viking Ship Hall at Bygdøy. The stem and stern were reconstructed after the ship had been moved; it was necessary to use some new material here, but as the stem and stern give the ship its character, this reconstruction must be said to be justified. Apart from the mast, which for good reasons could not be erected at its full height, the ship now appears in a "complete" condition.

14

The ship was built almost entirely of oak. Some of the smaller objects in the find were also of oak, and it was, on the whole, possible to treat these in the same way as the ship as far as preservation is concerned.

However, most of the other objects were made of softer woods. *Treatment by the* After extensive study and experiments it was found that the best *alum method* method of preserving these was by boiling them in a *strong solution of alum.* This made them quite brittle, but the method had a great advantage in that the fragments retained their original form so that they could be put together again. After being boiled in the alum solution, the fragments were impregnated with linseed oil, and finally given a coat of mat varnish.

All the *large* wooden objects were treated in this way. It was slow and laborious work, the actual alum treatment took a long time, and then the larger objects had to be pieced together from countless fragments. One of the sleighs for example, consisted of over a thousand fragments, and it took more than a year to complete it.

The years which have passed since this treatment was carried out have shown that even the objects that were boiled in an alum solution can deteriorate if they are kept for long in a room where the humidity changes frequently. At the exhibition of these objects at the Viking Ship Hall they are therefore mounted in show-cases in which the degree of humidity is controlled and changes are reduced to a minimum. In addition, the objects have been coated with modern oil-plastic varnish and a final coat of mat varnish to provide the necessary reinforcement.

The finest pieces of carving in the whole of the Oseberg find are *The preservation* the sleigh shafts and the so-called animal head posts. Of these, one *of the finest pieces* of the animal head posts was treated by the alum method, but this *of wood-work* proved to be unsuccessful as the finer details of the carving were partially obliterated. The other objects were therefore not treated to begin with, but were exhibited in large glass containers filled with water to which a little formaline had been added. In the first place this seemed to be a practical solution, but after a time it was found that the metal pins on several of the objects corroded, and ugly deposits of metal compounds were formed. When the question of exhibiting the find arose again after the war, it was clear that the

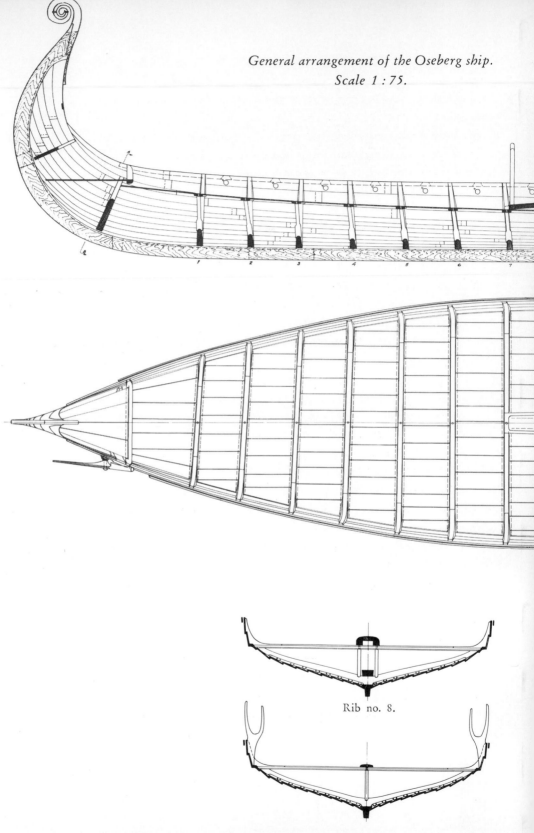

General arrangement of the Oseberg ship.
Scale 1 : 75.

Rib no. 8.

Rib no. 10.

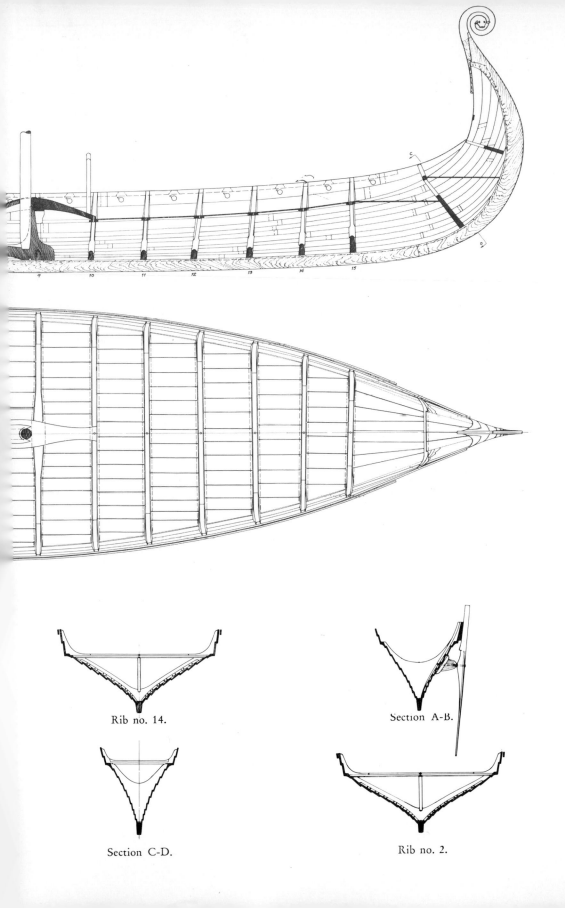

Rib no. 14.

Section A-B.

Section C-D.

Rib no. 2.

whole matter of conserving these very valuable, but in some cases badly preserved articles, would have to be considered seriously.

After considerable research and experiment, it was decided to use a completely new method which had been tried out in Denmark and also utilized in Switzerland with excellent results. The principle consisted in completely de-hydrating the objects by means of a special alcohol (trimethyl carbinol) which was then evaporated. Even though this sounds simple, it is a long and laborious process, but it seems to give good results.

After this treatment, the objects almost regain their original light wood tones, and become as light as cork. They are then impregnated with a plastic varnish, which certainly darkens them a little again, but the general effect is definitely much better than before. If they are then kept in air-conditioned glass cases, as at Bygdøy, it should be possible to preserve them for a long period provided that they are not subjected to any external influence.

*Exhibition*

The *exhibition* of the Viking ship finds has also given rise to difficulties, first and foremost of an economic nature. However, as further details concerning this are not of general interest, we shall confine ourselves to a brief outline of the history of the museum.

*The Viking Ship Hall*

The hall was planned as early as 1913, by Arnstein Arneberg, the architect, who was also the executive architect for the construction of the building. The wing for the Oseberg ship was completed in 1926 and the ship was moved there from the temporary shed in the University grounds. The next two wings for the Gokstad and Tune ships were opened in 1932, when all three ships were finally in place. The burial chambers from Gokstad and Oseberg were also exhibited in the Tune ship wing, but later the Oseberg chamber was removed to make room for two of the small boats from Gokstad, after they hade been restored.

At the outbreak of the last war, the fourth wing of the Viking Ship Hall, which was to house the objects from the Oseberg find, was still lacking. These objects had been provisionally exhibited on the first floor of the Historial Museum in 1912. In the autumn of 1939 they were removed to the cellar of the building for security reasons, and as further moves would be injurious, they remained here until they could be installed at Bygdøy.

18

*The reconstructed Oseberg ship, starboard side, viewed from the front in the Viking Ship Hall. Photo L. Smedstad.*

Work was not begun on the new wing until 1952, and in the New Year of 1957, the exhibits were transferred to Bygdøy. The installation was undertaken in the course of the spring, and the last part of the Viking Ship Hall was opened to the public.

The Viking Ship Hall was now complete as far as the ship finds were concerned; a new and practical vestibule was built simultaneously with the fourth wing and was opened in the summer of 1956, but the museum is still incomplete. According to the final plan it is to be extended further so that the entire University Museum of National Antiquities can be moved there. The collections are to be installed in new wings around the cruciform building of the Viking Ship Hall. The ship finds will thus be surrounded by the cultural environment from which they have sprung, and will literally form the mighty core of the museum's collections from the ancient past. But when this plan can be realized is still uncertain.

It is quite self-evident that a modern museum which houses irreplaceable cultural treasures must be adequately fire-proofed. This essential requirement was taken into consideration when the Viking Ship Hall was designed and built. The walls are of brick and concrete, and the floors of concrete; in the exhibition wings, they are paved with large slate flags. Since the external roof is of timber, parabular concrete vaults span the ceilings of the exhibition wings.

This construction was meant as an extra protection in case of fire, and on 12th June 1975, what we may literally term an ordeal by fire occurred: that evening, the wooden roof above the Gokstad ship wing caught fire. There were many people present, and the alarm was given right away. Even though the fire brigade arrived as quickly as possible, the fire had by then got a thorough hold of the timber construction, so that a great deal of heat was generated. But the vault proved able to stand the strain undamaged, and after a hectic struggle, the firemen were in control of the situation. The damage was confined to the external wooden roof, and none of the ships or of the other exhibits was damaged in any way. The architect's foresight saved some of our most irreplaceable cultural treasures on that occasion—of that we may be quite certain.

20

*The stern of the Oseberg ship, with the rudder; starboard side. Photo Mittet.*

## II. THE SHIP

*Description of the
Oseberg ship*

Like the ships from Gokstad and Tune, the Oseberg ship may be characterized as a large, open boat designed and equipped for both rowing and sailing. The ship is built entirely of oak, its full length was 21.58 metres, and it measured 5.10 metres at its broadest part; amidships the depth from gunnel to keel was 1.58 metres.

The Gokstad ship was a little larger and the Tune ship somewhat smaller, but the difference is so slight that all three must be said to belong to the same class of ship. They are smaller than the regular Viking long ship, and must have belonged to a group described in the sagas as "karvi", small vessels for the private use of chieftains and their followers for cruising along the coast. The Oseberg ship has the clear characteristics of a pleasure vessel for use in good weather on closed waters. The Gokstad and Tune ships are more in the nature of sea-going vessels, and are much more sturdily built, although the basic construction is the same in all of them. The description of the construction of the Oseberg ship, which is given below, applies in the main also to the other two, even though the Oseberg ship differs from them by its somewhat lighter build.

*The exterior*

The parts of the ship which are visible from the outside are the keel with the prow and stern, planking with the shield rack at the top, and the rudder. Then there is the inside of the ship: ribs, cross-beams with supports below, floor boards and supporting structure for the mast. In addition to the fixed equipment we have the mast, oars, gangway plank, bailer, cordage etc. With a crew of 35 men and all the necessary equipment, the ship's displacement has been calculated to be 11 tons.

*The keel*

*The keel* is 19.80 metres long. It is 25 cm deep in transverse section amidships, and the depth increases slightly towards the ends. The width is greatest amidships, 20 cm, and decreases to 13 cm at each end. An important feature in the formation of the keel is the gentle curve of the underside, made in such a way that is draws 30 cm more amidships than at the ends. In this way the greatest draught is where the hull is broadest, which increases the capacity of the vessel and makes it easy to turn.

The keel is made of two pieces which are joined by a so-called scarved joint 4 metres from the stern, that is, the two pieces to be

*Piece of wood-carving from the Oseberg ship. It is placed across the stern, just behind the helmsman's head.*

joined are bevelled so that they overlap, and are riveted with iron rivets.

Each side of the upper surface of the keel has a projecting batten to which the garboard strake is riveted. Towards the transition to the bow and stern, the projecting batten turns to a rabbet which continues along the bow and stern, and here the planks are nailed, not riveted.

Both the *stem and the stern* are made from beautiful, choice pieces of oak, and are fastened directly to the keel by scarved joints. The stem is made of a single piece of wood, as far as it has been preserved, but the stern has a joint, which presented the woodcarver with some difficulties when he was making the decorations on port side. *The stem and stern*

The top parts of both stem and stern were missing when the ship was found, but they were reconstructed after it was installed at Bygdøy, mainly on the basis of fragments that were preserved. As far as the stem was concerned, there were a number of reliable clues to be found, and the reconstruction here is probably fairly accurate. We know that the Viking ships could be identical at both ends, and it was therefore possible to reconstruct the stern on exactly the same lines as the stem apart from the final ornament which, on the stern, has the form of a tail complementing the serpent's head on the stem. Similar ornaments are known from illustrations of roughly the same period.

Joined to the keel, stem and stern is the *planking*. This consists of 12 strakes which are riveted together according to the ordinary principles of clinker-building: the garboard strake is placed with its edge under the keel's projecting batten, and each of the following *The planking*

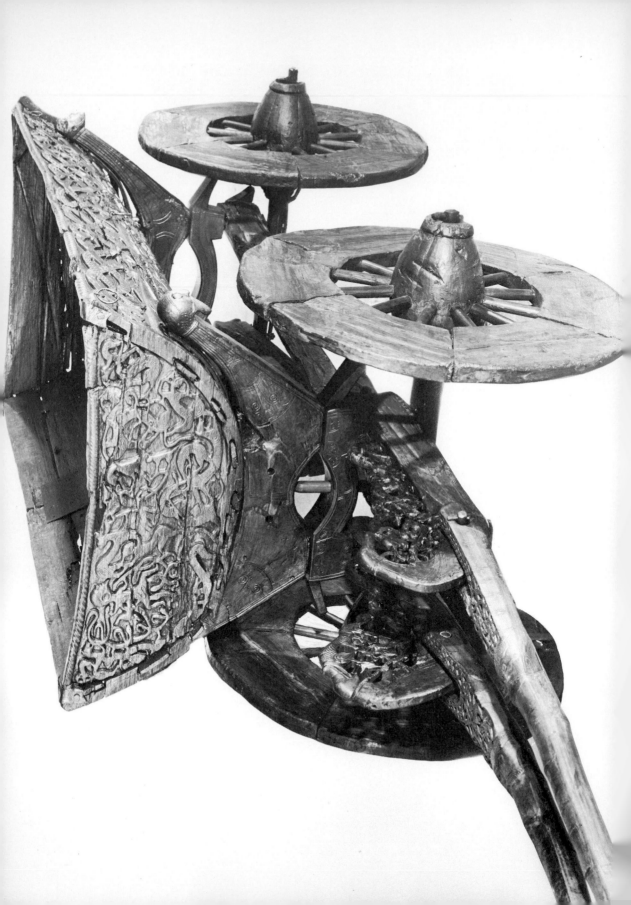

strakes is placed overlapping the one below. The strakes are held together by round-headed iron rivets driven through from the outside and secured by a small, square clinch plate on the inside.

The joints in the planking are made in the same way as in the keel, as scarved joints. In modern shipbuilding it is a fixed rule that these joints are made in such a way that the outer end points aft in order that the vessel may shed water as easily as possible when in motion. This is not the case throughout in the Oseberg ship, as some of the joints in the aft part of the ship face forward. The standard of craftsmanship in the vessel is otherwise so excellent that it is unlikely that this is due to carelessness or ignorance on the part of the shipwright, he must have had some reason for doing this, even though it is difficult for us to discover what it was.

Another ostensible defect in the ship is that it is partially "unbonded", that is to say that the joints in several overlapping planks lie directly one above the other. This is considered to be a weakness, but in the Oseberg ship it occurs only at the poop and the prow where the internal construction is so strong that there was no risk of weakening the side.

The first 9 of the 12 strakes form the bottom, the 10th the transition from bottom to sides, and the two last the free board, above the water. The width varies a little from strake to strake, and also on the individual strakes which are widest amidships and taper towards the ends. The thickness varies too: the bottom planks are on an average 2 cm thick, the two top strakes 2,5—3 cm, while the 10th strake has a different and particularly heavy shaping, because it constitutes a very important part of the construction.

The most remarkable feature of the planking is the way in which it is secured to the ribs. This is done by means of *lashing* through holes in the undersides of the ribs and corresponding holes in special cleats cut out from the strakes, directly under the ribs. The same method is also employed on the other Viking ships, although the material used for the lashing varies: narrow bands of whalebone were used on the Oseberg ship, fine spruce roots on the Gokstad ship, and thin bast twine on the Tune ship.

This method of construction appears out-of-date as well as cumbersome, and the shipwrights of the period certainly had other, simpler

*Joining of the planking to the ribs*

25

*Wood-carving on the Oseberg cart: detail from the front end of the body, probably representing Gunnar in the snake pit. Photo Ernst Schwitters, A.R.P.S., E.F.I.A.P. Universitetets Oldsaksamling.*

methods at their disposal. The ribs of the three small boats from the Gokstad find were secured to the strakes with tree-nails, a method which could also be applied to larger ships, as appears from the Klåstad ship as well as from the five Skuldelev ships. True, the latter are of somewhat more recent date than the Oseberg and the Gokstad ships, but according to the results of the radio-carbon analyses, the Klåstad ship must be roughly contemporaneous with ours.

Threads of tarred wool were pressed between the strakes for caulking, and thus the whole of the planking forms an unbroken skin, which is as thin and light as possible but sufficiently elastic to give a little when the ship forges through the waves. This point, however, is of greater importance in the Gokstad and Tune ships, which were built for heavier sailing than the Oseberg ship.

26

*Wood-carving on the Oseberg cart, left side.*
*Photo Ernst Schwitters, A.R.P.S., E.F.I.A.P. Universitetets Oldsaksamling.*

*The largest of the sleighs in the Oseberg find, during excavation. Note the ropes by which the body is lashed to the undercarriage. Photo Væring.*

Along the outside of the upper edge of the top strake runs a strip of pine which is secured by means of projecting cleats in such a way that there is a space of about 2 cm between it and the ship's side: this is the shield rack to which the shields could be fixed when the ship lay in port.

The oar-holes are placed under the shield rack, 15 on each side; the holes are round with an oblique slit slanting upwards and aft. The purpose of the slit is to enable the oarsmen to put the oars out from the inside, and they are placed in such a way that the sharp corners rubbed the oars as little as possible when the ship was rowed. There is no slit in the foremost oar-hole in each side: here the ship is too narrow for the oars to be put out from the inside, so there was no need for it.

28

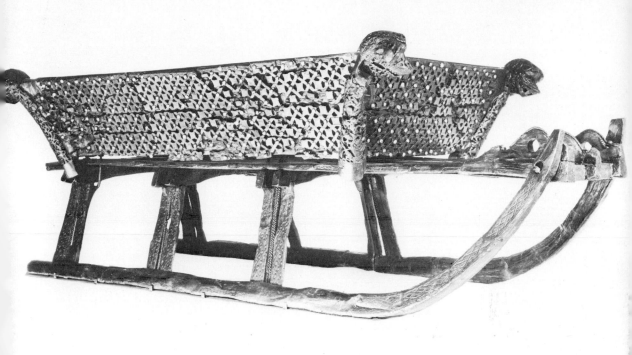

*The largest sleigh in the Oseberg find after restoration (cf. preceding illustration). Photo L. Smedstad.*

*The rudder* is shaped roughly like a large oar and is placed on the starboard side aft. It is held in place at the gunnel by a broad, plaited band of leather which could be undone easily. Further down the ship's side, it is fastened by a strong oak cleat. An elastic withe made from pine root is threaded through this cleat and a corresponding hole in the blade of the rudder, and is fastened to the so-called rudder rib inside. The elasticity of the withe makes it possible to turn the rudder on its own longitudinal axis by means of a tiller which is morticed into the neck of the rudder and projects into and across the ship.

As the rudder goes about 20 cm deeper than the keel, it was necessary that one should be able to raise it in shallow waters; the leather band on the gunnel was then undone and the rudder swung

29

up by means of a rope fastened to the heel. The Gokstad ship has a staple on the heel to which the rope was fastened, but this is omitted on the Oseberg ship.

*The interior: ribs and cross-beams*

With regard to the construction of the inside of the ship we have already mentioned *the ribs* in connection with the unusual way in which they are attached to the strakes. There are 17 ribs in the Oseberg ship, and a small "band" high up the stem and stern. Each rib is made from a strong piece of oak with a natural curvature corresponding exactly to the transverse section of the hull.

A strong *cross-beam* placed over each rib from end to end serves to strengthen the ship athwart, and also to provide a foundation for the deck, which rests on rabbets at the edges of the beams. In the middle the cross-beams are supported by *props* morticed to the underside of the beams at the upper end, while the lower end is cleft to sit astride the rib.

*The floor boards*

*The floor boards* are of pine, 2—3 cm thick, laid between the cross-beams in such a way that they form a continuous deck on a level with the 10th strake. Most of the boards were secured to the beams with tree nails, only a few were left loose for bailing purposes. The cavity under the deck was otherwise inaccessible.

At each end of the cross-beams there are brackets made of pieces of wood naturally grown at an angle. One arm is riveted to the upper side of the beam, the other arm sticks up almost vertically and served for securing the two top strakes on the side of the ship. The strakes are riveted to the arm with ordinary rivets.

*The keelson*

Finally we come to the pieces which carry and support the mast. First we have a large block of oak, "*the crone*" (or the keelson, as we would say today) which rests on the keel and houses the boot of the mast in a groove made for this purpose. This piece covers two ribs but has a comparatively slight support against displacement athwartships, only two cleats on each side. Above the "crone" the

*The mast partner*

mast is supported by the *mast partner,* a large piece of oak extending over four cross-beams. Although this piece was in rather a poor condition on excavation, its construction is clear enough. The mast partner is slightly curved longitudinally, so that it is raised as high as possible from the bottom. The fore part is massive and closed, but there is a groove aft to hold the mast when it was taken down.

30

*Wood-carving on the Oseberg cart: stylized male head.*
*Photo O. Holst.*

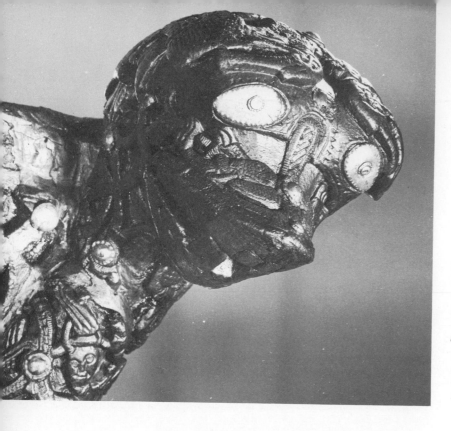

*Wood-carving on the largest sleigh in the Oseberg find. Animal head from one of the corner posts of the body.*
*Photo Ernst Schwitters, A.R.P.S., E.F.I.A.P. Universitetets Oldsaksamling.*

When the mast was raised the groove was closed with a block of oak, carved to fit it exactly.

The mast partner of the Oseberg ship has not such a marked fish-tail shape as those of the Gokstad and Tune ships, and is remarkably frail in comparison with them. It was, in fact, too frail for heavy sailing, as is clearly shown by the fact that there are ugly cracks in it which were repaired at the time with iron bands.

*The mast*

*The mast* is of pine and was 5.70 metres high when excavated, but was probably more than twice this length originally, about 13 metres. It is doubtful whether is was supported by fixed shrouds and stays.

Little remains of the attachments for the cordage inboard, and there was no trace of the sail, so that our knowledge about the sails and rigging is inadequate. It is certain that the ship had a large square sail, but we know no other details. A fair amount of cordage was found, but it does not seem at though this had anything to do with the rigging; it was probably used to draw the ship up from the

32

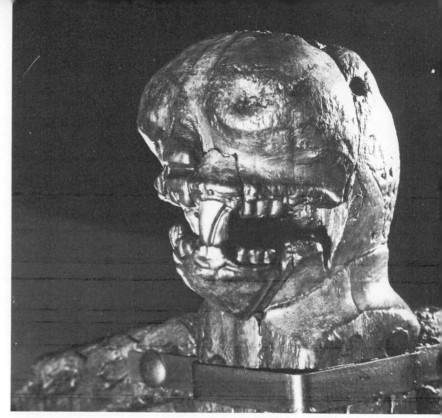

*Animal head on a corner post of the body of a sleigh in the Oseberg find.*
*Photo Ernst Schwitters, A.R.P.S., E.F.I.A.P. Universitetets Oldsaksamling.*

sea to the place where the barrow was to be raised and for the transport of material for the burial chamber.

Although the sail was lacking, all the 15 pairs of *oars* were found in the Oseberg ship, but they were obviously specially made for the burial. None of them shows any signs of wear, and several were not even completed. However, it is probable that they resemble the ship's original oars. All are made of pine and the length varies from 3.70 metres to 4.03 metres, all according to the distance between the oar holes and the surface of the water: this was greater at the bow and stern than amidships. *The oars*

The oars show a high standard of craftsmanship, and several of them bore traces of painted decoration. When the oars were not in use they could be stored in the large wooden forks which are placed in pairs on each side of the ship.

The oar holes are placed fairly low over the floor boards, so the crew must have sat while rowing. There were no thwarts or other fixed benches, and it is most probable that the rowers sat on loose

33

seats; perhaps they used their sea chests which were not part of the ship's equipment, but were taken ashore when the crew left the ship. This may be the explanation of the fact that none were found in the excavation of the Oseberg ship or the other two ships.

*The anchor and other equipment*

Here we shall mention only a few items among the equipment of the ship: *the anchor,* which is now exhibited under the bows is rather small and light — about 1 metre long and weighs just under 10 kilos. It is forged of iron to a very beautiful and graceful shape and is unusually well preserved. The *anchor stock* was made of oak, and is more than twice the length of the anchor; we do not know how they were attached to each other.

The *gang plank* was made of pine, 6.90 metres long and 30 cm broad, and now it lies in the ship. The underside is quite smooth, and there are 23 raised rungs cut from the upper side. There is a hole at one end so that it could be made fast to the ship when it was put out.

Finally, we would also mention the *bailer*. This is carved from a single piece of wood in the shape of a large, flat scoop with a fairly long handle for two hands. As we saw above, a few of the floor boards in the deck were loose so that it was possible to reach the bottom of the ship with the bailer.

*General charac- terization of the Oseberg ship*

In order to give a general characterization of the Oseberg ship, we must first repeat that it is comparatively fraily built, and its whole construction shows that it was *not* intended as an ocean-going vessel. The boards are very low in comparison to the size, and the structure that carries and supports the mast is of precariously slight dimensions.

We must assume that the Oseberg ship was not a utility craft, but rather a state vessel for a person of the chieftain class, almost what we would today call a yacht. This is also borne out by the fact that the craftsmanship is of a high standard and that much importance was attached to giving the vessel an impressive and elegant appearance. This was attained primarily by the strikingly high stem and stern, and the very fine wood-carving decoration found here. Closely corresponding carving may be seen on a number of objects in the rich grave-goods found onboard the vessel, and we shall therefore look more closely at this before trying to characterize the carving.

34

*The so-called «academic» animal head post in the Oseberg find.*
*Photo L. Smedstad.*

Before leaving the ship we would, however, point out that the wood carvings enable us to date the vessel to about or immediately after the year 800, that is, the very beginning of the Viking Age. The ship was, however, not new when it was buried. There are many indications, both in the ship itself and the objects found on it, that it was about 50 years old, that is to say that the burial took place in the middle of the ninth century.

## III. THE GRAVE FURNITURE

"Great folk are known by their riding equipment" says Peer Gynt. There was little riding equipment in the Oseberg find, but there was on the other hand *driving equipment* bearing the unmistakable stamp of the important people for whom it was made: a cart and three sleighs, all of them richly decorated with wood-carving. There was also a plain, undecorated working sledge, which will not be described here as it must be considered a farm implement rather than driving equipment.

*The cart* is in a class of its own, both in quality and size; its total length, including the shafts, is about 5.5 metres, the maximum width is about 1.5 metres and the height 1.20 metres. The construction itself is quite simple; the wheels are made of beech with heavy rims and hubs, while the spokes are somewhat lighter. They are connected with heavy axles joined to a centre bar forked at the rear; the ends of the fork are firmly secured to the rear axle, which is thus fixed in relation to the centre bar. Two large carved pieces of wood to which the shafts are attached are mounted on the front axle. The shafts are also decorated with wood carvings, but these are rather primitive and clumsy, especially in comparison with the extremely beautiful carving on the sleigh shafts.

The body of the cart rests on a pair of trestles which are joined to the centre bar with two small intermediary pieces of wood: the whole is held together by long, wooden bolts. The trestles which bear the body terminate in carvings in the shape of men's heads. naturalistic on the back trestle and stylized on the front.

The body is built as a box with a semi-circular cross-section. Each end consists of a single piece of wood completely covered with carved

36

decorations. The sides and the bottom are composed of 9 boards which are morticed into the ends and riveted together with iron rivets. The two upper boards on each side are decorated, while the others are plain.

The decoration of the cart differs in some respects from all the other wood-carving in the Oseberg find, but a close analysis would seem to show that it was executed by the same hand as the decorations on the ship. There are several indications suggesting that the cart may have been used for religious ceremonies and that it was a copy of an older cart of similar type. Because of the use to which it was to be put, the carver had to attempt to copy this earlier style, with which the craftsmen of the Oseberg period were not familiar.

*The cart: decoration*

The carving consists mainly of various kinds of animal figures, but among them we come across portrayals of human beings: small narrative scenes that to us have no comprehensible connection with the confusion of entwined and struggling animals with which they are surrounded.

The scene on the front-end is the most intelligible; it depicts a man struggling with snakes which surround him on all sides, while a four-footed beast bites him on one side. This probably illustrates the myth of Gunnar in the snake pit.

The scene roughly in the middle of the upper board on the right side is more difficult to interpret. It shows three people: a man is riding on horseback from the right and is met by another man who seizes the horse by the bridle with his left hand, while in his right he holds aloft something that must be meant to represent a sword. A woman is standing behind him, holding his right wrist as if to prevent him from striking. On both sides the human figures are directly connected with the ornamental animals that grip them at several points.

It may reasonably be assumed that this also depicts a scene from a saga or myth known to the Vikings, just as they were familiar with the story of Gunnar in the snake pit. Perhaps this is a scene from the Hiadings Myth—but we can do no more than surmise here.

*The sleighs*

*The sleighs* in the Oseberg find do not present us with the same problems as the cart. These, too, are replete with decorative carving, but this is all purely ornamental and falls more naturally into line with what we know from other sources about the artistic traditions of the Viking Age. The fact that the two main parts of which each sleigh consists, the undercarriage and the body, do not belong to each other is a different matter. The bodies were loose and were lashed to the undercarriages by means of ropes when the sleighs were in use, but they must have been mixed up at the time of the burial, for none of the sleighs has the body really belonging to it. Probably the largest sleigh has a body that originally belonged to one of the smaller ones, while these have bodies which do not fit any of the undercarriages.

The construction of the sleighs is very simple: when the body is removed they are not at all unlike ordinary, large, modern sledges. This is especially the case with the largest of them, which is 2.25 metres long and just over 0.80 metres at the widest part. In the Gokstad find we also have the remains of the undercarriage of a sleigh very similar to the largest of the Oseberg sleighs.

The other two sleighs are slightly smaller and otherwise rather similar in form. They are about 2 metres long and 0.76 and 0.85 metres wide respectively. Their construction differs from that of the large sleigh in that their runners are curved at both ends. The runners (and the uprights) are richly decorated with carvings, while the undersides are fitted with plain oak runners to protect the ornamental ones. The sleighs are made of beechwood. The plain runners follow the curve in front, but at the back they stop where the upward curve begins. There are no protective runners on the large sleigh, and the runners themselves are not decorated apart from a single entrelac band on the actual curve. The entrelac motive is also repeated on other parts of the undercarriage of this sleigh.

The bodies are built in an open box shape with sloping sides held together at the corners by solid corner posts terminated at the top with different forms of animal heads. On one of the bodies the corner posts have a square transverse section and have no ornaments apart from the animal head on top. This body is the oldest of the three, while the undercarriage on which it stands is one of the most recent, and probably belongs to the body which now stands on the largest sleigh.

38

*Detail from the carving on the "academic" animal head post in the Oseberg find. Photo E. I. Johnsen.*

In addition to the runners and bodies, the sleighs also have decorative carving on the boards on which the bodies rest, i.e. on those parts of the boards which project in front of and behind the body. Much of this carving is very interesting, but space does not permit us to go into details here. It should be noted, however, that the carving on the sledges was painted, so that certain parts were emphasized with individual colours. A few traces of colour still remained when the sleighs were excavated, but these could not be retained in the process of preservation, and have therefore almost entirely disappeared. This decoration is so involved that the colours may well have helped to make it make intelligible.

39

The fitting of iron spikes with tin-plated heads may, to some extent, have served the same purpose. Such spikes were put in in varying numbers—and with varying skill. As long as they are used sparingly they may serve to accentuate individual lines in the decoration. However they are used in increasing numbers and to some extent produce chaos rather than clarity. None of the sleighs as exhibited at present has its full complement of such spikes; many were missing and we have tried, as a rule, to show one side of a sleigh fully studded rather than to distribute the existing spikes evenly over the whole.

In spite of all the decoration found on the sleighs, it is clear that they are not purely ornamental. Although we know nothing of the use to which they were put, items such as the protective runners on the two smallest sleighs show that they were intended for driving, and not just for show.

*The sleigh shafts*

Another fact indicating that the sleighs had a "utility" purpose is the presence of three *sleigh shafts* in the Oseberg find. We do not know, however, to which sleigh each shaft belongs. The shafts were a little over 2 metres long when they were complete, and are decorated with some of the finest carving in the whole of the Oseberg find, thus forming a strange contrast to the simple and primitive carving on the shafts of the cart.

*The animal head posts*

The strange *animal head posts* comprise quite a different group of objects, but one that is closely related to the sleigh shafts in the matter of ornamentation. There were five of them in the find, but one of them was in very poor condition and can no longer be exhibited. However, the remaining four are all fairly well preserved, and the best of them, together with the sleigh shafts, constitute the very finest carving in the Oseberg find, and it is probable that they were carved by the same artists. The characteristics of the style and technique enable us to discern the work of one master who probably carved one animal head post and one sleigh shaft, and another who carved two of each.

It is not certain what these strange posts were used for, but all were found with metre-long wooden shafts that were morticed into holes at the base of the post. It therefore looks as if the animal head posts were carried by means of these shafts, which suggests

40

*One of the smaller sleighs in the Oseberg find. The undercarriage of this sleigh was probably originally made for the body now standing on the largest sleigh. Photo O. Holst.*

religious processions and other activities of this kind. They can scarcely have had any "practical" use. It is true that the corner posts on the bodies of the sleighs resemble the animal head posts in many respects, but it is highly doubtful that these were intended for a similar purpose.

We have now mentioned the majority and the most important of the objects ornamented with carving in the Oseberg find. Altogether it amounts to about 12—15 square metres, and it is obvious that it would be impossible to give a more detailed description. Nor is it necessary as it has already been done by Professor Shetelig in his excellent treatment of the subject in the third volume of the great work on the Oseberg find, an indispensable work for all who wish to study the object more closely. On the basis of a penetrating analysis of the style, he here shows how the material may be divided up into a series of different groups which he ascribes to the same

*The wood-carving in the Oseberg find*

41

number of "masters". The variation in the quality and style of the work is partly explained by the purely personal preference and skill of the individual masters, but partly also by differences in date.

It seems reasonable to assume that such vast and varied material as the wood-carving in the Oseberg find is not absolutely contemporaneous, and this is fully confirmed by closer study. It is not unreasonable to suppose that there may be a difference of half a century between the dates of the oldest and the most recent pieces of work (from the time around 800 to 850), but in spite of the dissimilarities they are all built up on a common basic motive—the animal figures. All the style or styles which we meet in this material form part of the animal ornamentation which had arisen long before the Oseberg period and was to continue long afterwards. In the course of this period, which stretched over several centuries, the animal ornamentation underwent a long period of development comprising a series of phases, some of which differ very much from others. The Oseberg find encompasses material from one of the most radical changes in this development: the transition between two stylistic phases which are now known as early and late Oseberg style. We shall touch on this question also in another connection.

*Metal work*

If the Oseberg grave had not been plundered in ancient times, *metal objects* of a style and quality comparable to that of the best examples of wood-carving would certainly have been found. This is not the case, however, no ornaments whatsoever of precious metal were found; there are a very few bronzes, and a number of iron objects. The latter show craftsmanship of a very high quality, not least because many of the objects are so unusually well preserved that every detail is as clear now as it was when it came from the smith's hand.

The iron objects are of no real interest as far as history of style is concerned, except for the so-called rattles with hooks. These iron implements have moulded bronze rings on the ferrule, decorated with the customary animal motifs which closely resemble some of the examples of wood-carving. Although these pieces of work are of very modest proportions, they are directly related to the monumental wood-carving and are thus of great importance for our comprehension of the art of the period.

42

The few remaining bronzes in the Oseberg find are rather small and of considerably less interest than the metal work from the Gokstad and Borre finds. First there are a number of small square plates for fixing on harness, adorned with a simple knot design. There are also a couple of strap mountings with animal motifs related to the designs on the most recent of the wooden objects.

While these small bronze objects are clearly native work, there *Imported bronzes* are also some pieces of metal work of quite another type; these, too, are small bronze ornaments, but the craftsmanship is in quite a different class, they are decorated with knife-sharp interlacing, and in one case with a small, elegantly drawn animal, altogether different from the more or less stylized and rough animal figures we meet in our native work.

It is clear that these bronzes are of foreign origin, and there is no doubt that they are western European. Quite a lot of Anglo-Irish metal work ornamented in the same style as that found in the Oseberg ship has been discovered in other Viking graves from more or less the same period.

And now we come to the most remarkable piece of metal work in the whole find, namely the mounts on the so-called "Buddha bucket". This is most probably of western European origin, and more likely Irish than British. The mounts are very different from the pieces of work that have been mentioned above.

The "Buddha bucket" is a wooden pail, made of strips of yew *The "Buddha* held together with brass bands. There is a band of the same metal *bucket"* along the rim, and the bucket was carried by a sturdy, moulded brass handle. The most remarkable thing about the bucket however, are the "ears" to which the handle is attached. They are identical and consist of a small, cast human figure with a comparatively large head and crossed legs, while the body consists of a rectangular tablet ornamented with blue, white, red and yellow enamel. The figure immediately calls a Buddha to mind, which is the reason why the pail is known as "the Buddha bucket"; it has retained this name even though it has not been possible to find any direct connection with Buddhist art.

All this work bears witness to a highly developed standard of craftsmanship—with regard to both the casting and the enamelling—

43

which must have been based on solid traditions. There was a rich tradition in enamel technique in Britain during the Viking Age, and British enamel work of a type very similar to that in the Oseberg find has been discovered in a couple of other Viking finds. These examples of enamel work appear together with plastic human figures or human heads which are so like the ones from Oseberg that we must consider them as being products of the same environment, "school" or tradition. The distinguishing feature of the Oseberg figures is the characteristic position of the arms and legs, precisely the traits which lead us to think of a Buddha. The question is whether the bronzecaster had such a model for his work, but to this we are unable to give an answer.

*Ornamental pails*

Of course we know nothing of the purpose for which this beautiful bucket was used, but it was scarcely an ordinary milk pail. The same may be said of another, larger bucket which is practically covered with brass bands. These so-called ornamental pails lead us to the many more ordinary buckets and pails and thus to the abundant selection of kitchen utensils in the Oseberg find.

*Ordinary buckets and pails*

To continue with the pails and buckets, four of these are more or less completely preserved, and there are fragments of others. A couple of them are equipped with handles, and one of these buckets is particularly well made, with brass bands and rim. Three large barrels should also be mentioned at the same time as the buckets, even though they may just as well be considered as ship's equipment; one of them is exhibited in the ship.

*Other kitchen equipment*

Many other wooden kitchen utensils were found. First we should mention a large trough (2.20 metres long), and 3 smaller ones, 5 dippers, 2 whole and 2 fragmentary dishes, and finally one undamaged wooden bowl, and the remains of a several others.

A small kitchen stool is also included in the kitchen equipment, as well as two choppers and a long knife, all with wooden handles. And these bring us to the ironwork, which we touched on above: in this group we have two cauldrons, together with a tripod on which to hang a cauldron, and a pot-hanger, also fragments of a third cauldron. Apart from the cauldrons, which were partly damaged, the ironwork is unusually well preserved and the pot-hanger in particular is a fine specimen of the smith's art.

*Wood-carving on one of the sleighs in the Oseberg find. Photo O. Holst.*

A couple of large lamps may be mentioned together with these iron goods, even though they are not necessarily part of the kitchen equipment; both consist of a wide iron bowl mounted on a long, perpendicular iron rod which is partly twisted and pointed at the end. There is a frying pan of the type common in the Viking Age, a small, flat pan and long, straight iron handle, and a grinding stone. With these, mention has been made of almost all the kitchen equipment.

The rest of the *household goods* should now be described: the most striking of these are the beds, particularly the larger one which

*Remaining household goods: furniture*

45

has head posts topped by carved animal heads. The inside length of this bed is only 1.65 metres, while the width is 1.80 metres. The two other beds which were found are smaller and simpler, more like modern beds. Unfortunately all three were in such poor condition that is was impossible to reconstruct them, but a full-sized copy has been made of each. Here we must mention the four bed staffs, even though we are not certain that they were used as their name implies. Other "furniture" besides the beds includes first of all the chair, which is small and box-shaped with a simple, flat back.

The chests form part of the furniture as well, and fortunately at least two of them are better preserved: a third chest had been seriously damaged, and there are a great many fragments of other chests. The chest which is best preserved is particularly handsome: it is reinforced with broad iron bands held in place by iron spikes with large, tin-plated heads. The lock hasps are examples of fine wrought-iron work.

*Textile implements*

The tools for women's work are closely connected with the furniture and should almost be considered as part of it: most of them are implements for the making of textiles. The looms are the largest and most striking objects here, but they are, unfortunately, in poor condition. Altogether we have the more or less complete remains of four looms: one slightly damaged ribbon weaver's loom, and fragments of another, a loom which was most probably used for weaving narrow tapestries, and a piece which is thought to be the foot of a fourth loom. The reason why they are in such poor condition is that they, together with the rest of the household goods, were placed in the burial chamber and were roughly treated by the robbers.

In addition to the looms, we also have a number of smaller textile tools. First we must mention two sets of tablets, one complete and one defective, for the weaving of ribbons and belts. The complete one consists of two small wooden rods together with 52 small square tablets, of thin wood, each with a hole at all four corners. A half-finished ribbon was still in this loom, which was found in a bed in the fore-part of the ship. 38 square tablets for a similar loom were found in the burial chamber, together with a couple of wooden pins, which probably also belonged to it.

46

*One of the "baroque" animal head posts in the Oseberg fin*
*Photo L. Smedsta*

Other textile tools which were found include a spindle whorl for spinning woollen thread, wooden clubs and flax beaters, wooden needles, a pair of iron scissors of normal Viking Age design, fragments of a yarn-winder, together with what is thought to be two yarn reels. A number of other small implements for textile work and a comb made of bone were found in a couple of wooden boxes, which had been used as sewing caskets. Here we may mention that remnants were also found of a couple of caskets which had brass fittings, iron hinges and clasps. Of more personal belongings, apart from the comb already mentioned, two other combs were found, in two different chests. There were also two pairs of shoes of thin leather and some remnants of shoes.

*Personal effects*

Finally we must mention a wooden saddle, which belongs to the personal effects rather than to the driving equipment.

*Agricultural implements*

Besides the very varied equipment for indoor work, the Oseberg find also contained a large, but far less varied number of articles for farm work. First comes the simple working sled which is constructed on more or less the same lines as the largest of the decorative sleighs, and is of the same size but without any form of ornamentation. The sled was in such poor condition that it was impossible to piece it together again; instead, a copy has been made of the undercarriage.

The agricultural implements also include the wooden spades, dung fork and the two hoes. There are two types of spades, one of which has a little ledge on which to rest the foot. However, we must at once make it clear that these cannot be reckoned as part of the original grave-goods: most of them must have been used by the robbers, and the remainder for the building of the barrow.

In addition to the many easily recognizable implements found in the Oseberg ship, we have also a number of small objects such as wooden pins, ropes, and a large number of fragments which are difficult to identify, and there is no point in giving an account of them here. Before we finish our account of the Oseberg find, however, a few words must be said about the remnants of textiles that were excavated. These provide one of the most important discoveries in the whole find, but the scientific treatment of the material has not yet been published, and for this reason we shall only mention briefly a few of the main features.

*The «Buddha bucket» in the Oseberg find.*

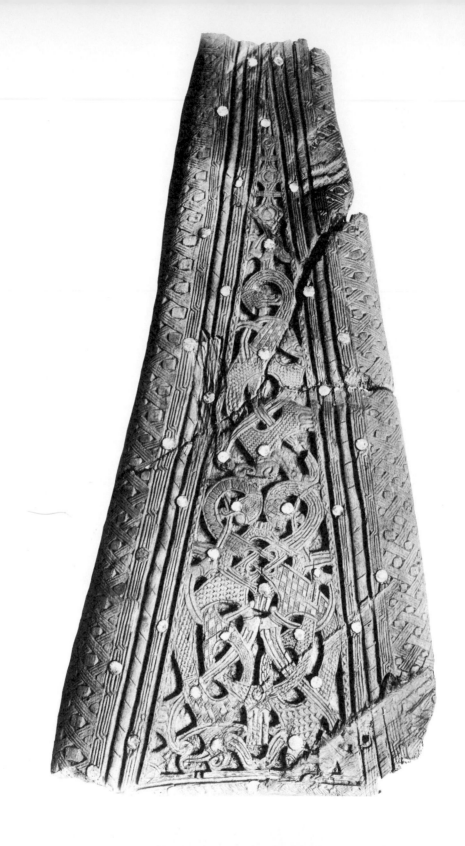

Most of the textile remnants were found in the burial chamber, and had been pressed together into hard "cakes" which it has been a long and difficult job to disintegrate. In some cases they were also stuck in large lumps of feathers, which undoubtedly came from the beds in the burial chamber.

The textiles are made of wool and silk, but there is no trace of linen; this must be due to the conditions in the mound, as we know that flax was cultivated and made into linen in this country in Viking times, and there are tools for linen work in the Oseberg find. Of the other materials, the silk must have been imported, while the wool is native work, with the probable exception of a woollen material of particularly fine quality.

Among the woollen materials are found a few sparse remains of garments as well as fragments of tapestry, and it is the latter group that is most interesting to us although it is not easy to make out what they represent. In the first place the material has largely lost its original colouring, so that contrasts now consist largely of different shades of brown and grey. An even greater difficulty is that the work has disintegrated into many small pieces, and it is impossible to find any real connection in the pictures.

The Oseberg tapestry is very different from what we normally understand by tapestries, in size as well as technique: it consists of the remnants of very narrow, but probably quite long friezes, possibly wall hangings, 16 to 23 cm in width; of course we know nothing of their length. Naturally they seem very small to us, but in spite of their modest proportions they are filled with an incredible number of human and animal figures. We find large processions of people, walking, riding and driving, and every space between the figures is filled with smaller ones: spears, swastikas, knots and birds, to mention the most important.

It is, of course, almost impossible to say what the different pictures are meant to portray, as the material is so fragmentary; but as far as one can see, religious activities as well as historical motives are illustrated. We are on safer ground with the information with which the pictures can provide us concerning cultural history, for example with regard to the history of dress. Here we can learn a great deal, more, in fact, than we can learn from the remnants of the actual

51

*Detail from the carving on one of the sleigh shafts in the Oseberg find.*

clothes which were also found. And last, but not least, they teach us a great deal about the art and technique of tapestry weaving in Viking times: enough to enable us to say that the weavers were as skilfull in their field as the wood-carvers were in theirs—they mastered their materials and their medium with equal assurance and excellence. We can scarcely give them higher praise.

At this point we leave the Oseberg find. The description that has been given of it aims in no way at being exhaustive, the find is too large and singular for this. Instead the intention has been to give some information and comments which, it is to be hoped, will provide a useful supplement to a visit to the Viking Ship Hall.

But the Viking Ship Hall does not contain only the Oseberg find: three other Viking ship finds are also exhibited, and a few words must be said about them too. The Oseberg find certainly takes the pride of place among the Viking ship finds, and has therefore been described most exhaustively; there is no doubt that the Gokstad find holds the second place, and we shall therefore continue there.

# THE GOKSTAD FIND

In the summer of 1880, the Gokstad ship was excavated on the land of the Gokstad farm in the modern borough of Sandefjord. Like the Oseberg ship, the Gokstad ship had also been covered by a very large barrow measuring 43—50 metres across and about 5 metres in height. Originally it may have been even larger, but it had been somewhat reduced by cultivation. Nicolay Nicolaysen, antiquarian and archaeologist, who excavated more barrows than anyone else, was responsible also for this excavation.

*The Gokstad ship: the excavation*

The barrow was built of clay mixed with sand, while the greater part of the ship was buried in the subsoil of blue clay. The ship had also been filled with blue clay at the time of the burial, and here, as in the case of the Oseberg ship, the clay had preserved the woodwork very well. Fortunately for us, part of the upper sections of the ship had also been pressed down into the blue clay by the weight of the barrow; the parts that projected over the blue clay had decayed completely, first and foremost the stem and stern, and also almost all of the two upper strakes with the gunnel. The burial chamber, on the other hand, was in good condition, as it consisted of sturdy, round timbers covered by several layers of birch bark.

As in the Oseberg find, the burial chamber had been erected in the aft part of the ship, and here were found the remains of the skeleton of a man. This grave had, however, also been plundered in ancient times, and the goods in the burial chamber were therefore rather few. A Viking Age man's grave is almost certain to yield weapons, just as the undisturbed grave of a woman will contain jewelry. However, there were no weapons in the Gokstad grave just as the Oseberg grave was without jewelry. In both cases the reason must be grave robbery.

*The burial chamber*

The contents of the burial chamber on the Gokstad ship are easily enumerated: a few remnants of textiles (wool and silk) probably

53

part of the apparel of the dead man, fragments which most likely were the remains of a bed, a gaming board with one antler gaming piece, some bits of leather which may have been a purse, a socketed iron point, the clasp of a casket and three iron fishing hooks together with a large number of metal harness mounts (iron, lead, bronze gilt).

*Finds outside the burial chamber*

*Outside the burial chamber,* in the aft part of the ship, a number of objects were found, among them some logs and timbers, an iron cauldron and a pot hook, a wooden bucket, six cups of hardwood and an oak plate. The tiller of the ship was also found here, and last, but not least, we must mention the skeleton and parts of the plumage of a *peacock.*

The skeletons of a number of other animals were found *outside the ship,* viz. at least twelve horses and six dogs. Here were also discovered the blade of an oar and some iron implements: two augers and a palstave or celt as well as a small axe blade.

Most of the grave furniture was found in the fore part of the ship, between the prow and the burial chamber. Among the largest objects we must mention three small boats, the remains of five beds and a sixth bed with carved animal heads on the head boards, which were first taken to be the remains of a high seat, the verge boards of a tent (also with carved animal heads, rather similar to those on the bed posts), a number of oars and, finally, the remains of a sleigh. A multitude of logs and timbers may also be mentioned here. The ship's anchor stock is in a class of its own; it is of oak, and very well preserved, while all that remains of the anchor itself is a lump of rust. The only other metal object found here was a large cauldron of copper or bronze. Here there was also a large keg, which presumably held the ship's supply of drinking water. Only a few kitchen utensils were found: some chopping boards, a trough, and a couple of wooden plates. Then there was a part of a wooden vessel which may have been the ship's bailer, and finally a lot of rope and some fragments of textiles.

*General characterization of the Gokstad find*

Altogether, the number of objects or fragments of objects found here was quite large, but there was nothing that can be compared with the best of the wood-carving in the Oseberg find. On the whole the objects are simpler and to some extent they were in a poorer condition, they were not subjected to the same treatment for

*The Gokstad ship photographed during excavation, viewed from the front, starboard side. The gables of the burial chamber can be seen in the aft part of the ship.*

preservation and restoration as the contents of the Oseberg find, after the excavation. Only on one directly comparable point are the grave goods from Gokstad of greater interest than those from Oseberg, and that is where the small pieces of decorative metal work are concerned. And then there are the small boats which have no counterparts at all in the Oseberg find or any other Norwegian find from the Viking Age. When we finally come to the *ship* itself, we find that it is far superior to that from Oseberg, even if the superfical impression it gives is more sober and less ostentatious.

*The Gokstad ship: dimensions and construction*

The main features of the construction of the Gokstad ship are similar to those of the Oseberg ship, and therefore any detailed description is unnecessary: it should be sufficient to indicate some of the points where they differ from each other. In the first place the Gokstad ship is a little larger, it was built for 16 pairs of oars, whereas the Oseberg ship was built for 15 pairs. It is 23.24 metres long between the extreme points, the maximum beam is 5.20 metres, and the height from the bottom of the keel to the gunnel amidships is 2.02 metres. The weight of the hull, fully equipped, is estimated at 20.2 metric tons; an exact copy of the ship that was built in 1893 had a tonnage of 31.78 register tons.

In addition to its larger dimensions, the Gokstad ship is also distinguished by a more sturdy construction throughout, which made it far more seaworthy. But like the Oseberg ship it is a *"karvi"*, a fairly small vessel for cruising along the coast. That it also had sea-going qualities was fully demonstrated in 1893 when an exact copy was sailed across the Atlantic to be displayed at the World Exhibition in Chicago. The captain of the ship, Magnus Andersen, who was later appointed Director of Shipping and Navigation, has given a detailed account of and paid high tribute to the seaworthiness of the ship in his book "Vikingfærden"; this praise must apply equally to the original.

*The exterior*

Outwardly, the greater strength of the Gokstad ship is firstly due to the considerably greater height, and secondly to the far stronger keel. The latter is cut in one piece without any joints, and has a remarkably high, clear-cut transverse section: the idea behind this was clearly to combine the greatest possible strength with the least

56

*The reconstructed Gokstad ship, viewed from the front in the Viking Ship Hall.*
*Photo Mittet.*

possible weight. As in the Oseberg ship, the bottom of the keel forms a flat, even curve, drawing deepest exactly amidships.

The Gokstad ship is also built entirely of oak, and the keel gives us an idea of the oak material which the shipbuilders of that time had at their disposal. Forestry experts have calculated that it required a straight grown oak about 25 metres high. When the copy of the ship was to be built in 1893, the keel was made of Canadian oak, as it was impossible to find any serviceable material in this country.

The stem and stern are made of choice oak joined to the keel by means of short transitional pieces. They are very strong, but unfortunately we know nothing of the form of the upper parts as these had rotted away in the barrow. No attempt has been made on the reconstructed ship to show how the stem and stern were terminated, and the new parts have a slightly lighter tone than the original, so that it is possible to see at once what is new and what is old. This has also been done with the upper strakes and in all other places where it was necessary to put in new material.

In the Gokstad ship, the actual hull has a much rounder form in transverse section than that of the Oseberg ship, and the sides are also somewhat higher: they consist of 16 strakes compared with 12 on the Oseberg ship, and two of these are above the oar holes. As in the Oseberg ship, the strake which forms the transition between the bottom and the side of the ship is much more strongly made than the bottom strakes, and the same applies to the strake with the oar holes. The latter could be shut by small shutters on the inside when the ship was under sail, otherwise they have the same form as those on the Oseberg ship, with slits for the oar blades.

The top strakes are particularly thin and are supported by special top ribs. Here, in contrast to the Oseberg ship, the shield rack is fixed inside the ship. When the ship lay in port it could be adorned with shields which were hung up outboard along the gunnel and fastened to the shield rack with thin cords, in such a way that they half overlapped one another. There were two shields between each pair of oar holes, that is 32 along each side. At the time of the excavation the remains of all 64 shields were found along the sides of the ship, painted alternately yellow and black. The shields were round, about one metre in diameter, and were made of quite thin

*Interior from the Gokstad ship.*
*Photo Ernst Schwitters, A.R.S.P., E.F.I.A.P. Universitetets Oldsaksamling.*

wood. In the middle there is a shield boss of iron to protect the hand; the grip is fixed across the boss on the inside. One of the shields from the Gokstad ship is hung up under a couple of verge boards from the same find on the gable wall of the Oseberg wing of the Museum. Another pair of verge boards hangs on the gable wall of the Tune ship wing.

*The interior*

The Gokstad ship also differs on some points where the fittings inside the ship are concerned. In the first place there are the top ribs, which have already been mentioned. Further, the mast partner and "crone" (keelson) have a much stronger construction so that they could really stand the strain of a rough trip. Here the floor boards are not riveted on, but lie loose so that the space underneath could be used for stowing away those things which were not needed on deck. There were also three large uprights for the same purpose, one of these is nailed on to the mast partner, just before the mast; .the other two, one in the middle of the fore part of the deck and the other in the middle of the after-deck, were loose and could be raised or taken down as required.

*General charac-
terization of the
Gokstad ship*

In general, we may say that the Gokstad ship, to a far greater extent than the Oseberg ship, bears the characteristics of a practical utility vessel. There is only one single example of ornamentation, but this is of high quality and consists of a carved animal head on the tiller: at present the ship has a copy of this, as the original was not sufficiently well preserved. Otherwise the Gokstad ship is devoid of all decoration, but is in no way inferior to the Oseberg ship in the high standard of craftsmanship that has gone into its making. In stability, serviceable construction and building, it is, in fact, superior. Perhaps this is a result of the progress which must have been made during the interval between the building of the two ships. The Gokstad ship was probably built about or just after the middle of the ninth century, roughly half a century after the Oseberg ship. The first of the Viking expeditions took place at this time, and it is only natural that the experiences gained at sea should result in visible improvements in shipbuildings methods and construction.

*The small boats
from the Gokstad
find*

The *small boats* from the Gokstad find are also characterized by high technical quality and craftsmanship. We saw above that there

60

*The Gokstad ship in the Viking Ship Hall, seen from the front, a little to port side.*

GOKSTADSKIBET

*Interior of the Gokstad ship: the stern with the high poop and the rudder.*
*Photo Ernst Schwitters, A.R.P.S., E.F.I.A.P. Universitetets Oldsaksamling.*

were three of them, all made of oak and of slightly varying sizes: 9.75, c. 8.00 and 6.60 metres long. The largest and the smallest have been restored and are exhibited in the Tune ship wing of the Viking Ship Hall. They were rowed by three and two pairs of oars respectively, and the medium sized boat also had two pairs of oars. Probably only the smallest can be regarded as a ship's boat, while the other two are part of the grave furniture.

62

*The stern and rudder of the largest of the Gokstad boats. Note the similarity to the construction of the rudder of the ship. Photo Ernst Schwitters, A.R.P.S., E.F.I.A.P. Universitetets Oldsaksamling.*

It is tempting to compare these three boats with the three ornamental sleighs in the Oseberg find. The interests of the Gokstad chieftain lay clearly more in the direction of travel by sea than by land, and the craft he was given are just as impressive at the sleighs in the Oseberg find as far as elegance and quality of craftsmanship are concerned. Once more we see the same characteristic difference between these things as we found between the ships in

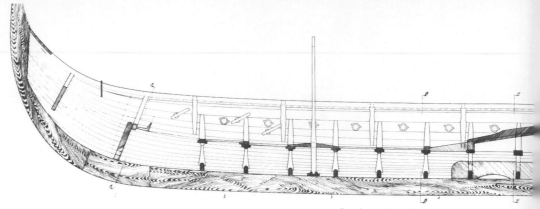

Section through central line.

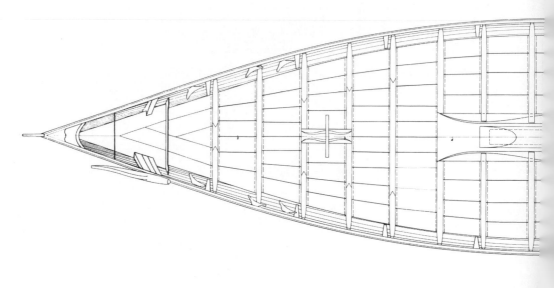

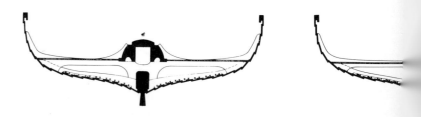

Section C-C.

*General arrangement of the Gokstad s[*

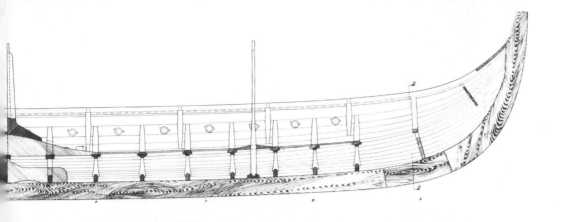

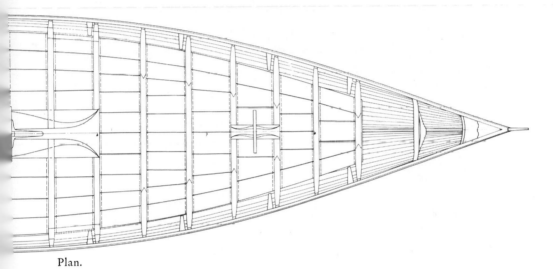

Plan.

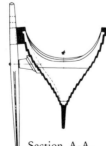

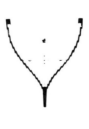

ion B-B.　　　　　　Section A-A.　　　　　Section D-D.

*le 1 : 80.*

*Decorative carving from the Gokstad find.*

the two finds: on the one hand magnificent decoration, on the other severe simplicity combined with well-nigh functional perfection.

Besides their unusually beautiful and elegant lines, what primarily characterizes these boats is their light construction. On the largest, which is actually quite a big boat, the planking is only 8—15 millimetres thick. The boat has only one fixed cross-piece, and the ribs, too, are rather slender. In the small boats the planking is attached to the ribs by tree-nails, not lashings, as in the ships. Finally we must note that the small boats are equipped with rudders of the same construction as those on the ships, placed on the side, and that they were rowed by means of rowlocks with grommets. With their slender, elegant form they must certainly have been able to make good speed when rowed by experienced oarsmen, but at the same time they were rather easily capsized.

*The Burial chamber* from the Gokstad ship is displayed in the Tune ship wing. It has a form similar to a large ridged tent and was erected directly aft of and adjoining the mast. It is mentioned here because one aspect of it is particularly interesting: it shows us the oldest example of bonding technique preserved in this country. The lower part of the chamber consists of a framework two timbers high, bonded together at the corners. Otherwise the whole structure is quite simple and primitive, as it was not intended that it should ever be seen again. The grave robbers had entered the chamber on the port side and even hewn out a large piece of the solid framework. A piece is missing from the raftered roof here, too, so that there is a large, gaping hole along the whole of one side of the burial chamber.

*The burial chamber from the Gokstad find*

Because of the dissimilarities between the Oseberg and Gokstad finds, they form excellent complements to each other, not least in the field of the history of style. True enough, the sober-minded Gokstad chieftain had little decorative wood carving with him, only a few carved animal heads: the plastic head on the tiller and the flat heads on the bed posts and the verge-boards. These flat heads have direct parallels in the Oseberg find, and represent a later stage of development of the animal heads found on the bed posts and verge-boards there.

The Gokstad find is, on the other hand, compensated by its

*Metal work*

67

*decorative metal work*. As pointed out above, many metal *mountings* were found in the burial chamber, and when the Gokstad barrow was reassembled in the 1920-ies, a few more small pieces of metal work were discovered, some of them quite similar to the first. Most of the metal work consists of harness mountings, the majority of them being rather small. The greatest number are made of lead, and have a comparatively simple design. The bronze work is much more interesting, most of the pieces are gilded. In a few cases we meet almost naturalistic representations: a horseman with a spear and an animal which is probably meant to be a lion. Otherwise the work is purely ornamental, and consists either of interlacing or animal motifs, or a combination of both. This metal work was of great importance for a secure dating of the find, and takes us back to the time round about 900.

The animal motifs we meet in the small pieces of bronze work from the Gokstad find are very distinctive. Their style is based on that of the most recent pieces of work in the Oseberg find, but it had developed so much that it must be considered as a style of its own. It is generally known as the *"Borre style"* after the Borre find, which will be described at the end of the book, and where it is well represented. In the meantime we must first consider the third Viking ship: the Tune ship.

This find, unlike the Oseberg and Gokstad finds, comprises very little beyond the ship itself, which was excavated in 1867 on Lower Haugen farm at Rolvsøy (at that time in the parish of *Tune*) a few kilometres north of Fredrikstad. This is on the eastern side of the Oslo fjord, while both the other finds lay on the western side. Responsible for the excavation was this country's first professor of archaeology, Oluf Rygh.

As the ship now stands in its wing of the Viking Ship Hall, it seems very unimpressive compared with the other two. Not only is it somewhat smaller, but no attempt has ever been made to restore it. Apart from a few thin iron bands to keep the planking together, the ship has more or less the same appearance as when it was excavated.

All the main features of construction of this ship were the same as for the other two. It is built of oak, while the rudder and the cross-beams are made of pine, and the props under the cross-beams are lacking, probably because these are so short that support cannot have been necessary. The ship measured about 4.35 metres across at its widest part; its present length is roughly 15 metres, but its original length was much more, probably about 20 metres. The stem and stern have rotted away, to there is no way of telling its full length.

*The Tune ship: dimensions and construction*

The upper strakes have also been lost, so the ship appears to be still lower than it actually was. The height from the bottom of the keel to the gunnel is estimated at 1.20 metres (0.82 m less than on the Gokstad ship). This has given the Tune ship a character of its own, quite different from the Gokstad ship; more flat-built, shallow and very little freeboard. The width appears to be out of all proportion to the depth, but this must have been necessary to make for sufficient stability when under sail: the particularly sturdy construction of the mast partner and "crone" show that this ship was intended for real sailing.

69

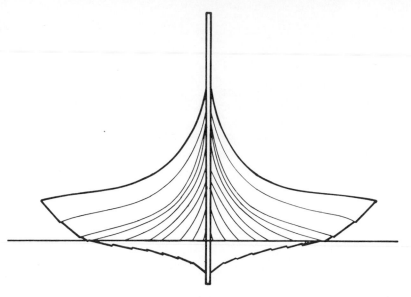

*Reconstruction drawing of the Tune ship. Front view.*

As the upper strakes in the planking are missing we cannot be sure how many pairs of oars there were, probably 11 or 12. No oars were found during the excavation, however.

There was very little of what could be described as grave furniture, the most important are a few fragments of a wooden object with carving in high relief, a couple of glass beads, a few pieces of textile and the blades of a few ordinary wooden spades. Nothing but traces of rust remained of the iron, but among these it was possible to distinguish the grip of a sword, something that may have been a spear-head and a shield boss. The only clue to the age of the find are the pieces of carving which suggest the latter half of the 9th century, that is about the same period as the Gokstad ship.

*Dating the vessel*
In quality and craftsmanship the Tune ship is fully up to the standard of the other two, and the conditions in the find were also more or less the same: the ship was enclosed in a large barrow with blue clay in the subsoil. On the other hand the burial chamber differed from the others in that the long walls were rammed into the clay *outside* the gunnel, probably as there was insufficient room inside the ship. Only a few pieces of planks remain of the burial chamber, so we have no secure knowledge of its appearance.

# THE BORRE FIND

On one important point the outward circumstances of this find were the same as in the other three: a ship enclosed in a large barrow and, as far as can be seen, originally well equipped with grave furniture. In this case the mound was a long barrow, while the others were more or less round, but a yet more important distinction is that the Borre mound did not provide the same conditions for the preservation of woodwork. Here the barrow consisted mainly of sand or gravel, and the "excavation" was undertaken by the highways authorities who used the mound as a sand or gravel pit from 1850—52. The find was therefore very badly taken care of, and we must assume that much of the grave furniture was lost.

*Conditions in the find*

Of the ship itself, barely more than the rivets and nails remain, so we know very little about it. There are not many other wooden objects: a few pieces which most likely originate from a saddle, and others which *may* be the remains of a cart or sleigh shaft, but it is impossible to be certain. The latter objects are richly studded with metal mountings. There is also a large number of small metal mountings for harnesses, as in the Gokstad find, and some of them are closely related to these. Of particular interest are some side-pieces for bits. Here we should also mention a terret of bronze gilt.

*The find: the ship and grave furniture*

Most of these mountings are of bronze gilt, decorated in a very characteristic style which has been given the name *"Borre style"* after this find. Here, as in the Oseberg style, we find animal decorations, a later development of the style of the most recent objects from Oseberg, although pure interlacing motifs also play quite an important part. As pointed out above, we here have objects in exactly the same style as in the Gokstad find, which leads us to believe that these finds are more or less contemporaneous: from the period about the year 900.

*Dating the find*

We can safely say that the ornamental metal work constitutes the most important of the material from the Borre find. But in addition

71

to these we must also mention a strange glass goblet, a tangible proof of connections abroad, as it is probably Frankish work. An iron stirrup and axe blade are certainly of native origin, and other iron goods include a cauldron and pot-hook, as were also found at Oseberg and Gokstad, although these are unfortunately in a very bad condition. All the most important things have been mentioned when we include a large bead of rock crystal and a soapstone spindle whorl as well as the remains of the skeleton of a horse.

*General charac-*
*terization*

Compared with Oseberg and Gokstad, the Borre find does not seem particularly impressive. In the first place the ship is lacking, due to the unfavourable conditions for its preservation. There certainly was a ship, and the sparse remains of the grave goods show clearly enough that the burial chamber was well equipped. It is therefore quite logical to couple this find to the "big three", more especially so as objects from it are exhibited in the wing occupied by the Oseberg collection.

The fact that the find was discovered at Borre is of particular interest, but we shall return to this at the end, in connection with the importance which the ship finds have for our national history. But first we must consider their significance for our cultural history.

## THE SIGNIFICANCE OF THE VIKING SHIP FINDS

It is obvious that the Viking ship finds are of enormous importance to our knowledge of that strange period of Norwegian history known as the Viking Age. We begin to realize exactly *how* important they were when we turn the question around and try to imagine how much poorer we should be without them.

The question is most easily answered where purely cultural history is concerned, and the *ships* themselves naturally take a prominent place in the picture. The introduction includes an account of the importance of these finds with regard to our knowledge about Viking Age ship building. The only thing now lacking is the knowledge of how the ships were used: we do not know with certainty how the crew sat while rowing, nor do we know much about the sail and how it was used. *The Viking ships*

We know a great deal about the technique of ship building, on the other hand. We recognize the high standard of craftsmanship, and by comparing the ships we are able to see clearly that we have here a firmly established and reliable "school" of shipwrights. A feature such as the manner in which the ribs were secured to the strakes—by lashing—proves this. In all other known Viking ships, the ribs were secured with tree-nails. Such a school is founded on tradition, and it is manifest that these ships are not the work of beginners in the art. From the rock carvings we know that ships have been built and used along our coasts at least as far back as the Bronze Age (about 1500—500 B. C), and from the Iron Age we have a series of finds which show us some of the stages of development towards the Viking ships. We see how some things caused particular difficulties, primarily the stem and stern and the keel. But in the Viking ships these problems have been solved, and in fact the highest stage of development possible in this field has been reached. The Gokstad ship is a perfect example of an open boat of its size, equipped for both sailing and rowing. Even so, there were still possibilities for further development. Larger ships could, for instance, be built, and we learn from literature that ships of up to twice the size were built in the Middle Ages. Further, there were possibilities for differentiation in the various types of ships built for special purposes, and thus other technical solutions could be considered. This supposition is confirmed by the finds of ships from Skuldelev and by our own Klåstad ship. Thus our three "old" Viking ships represent one phase in a long process of development, but it was an extremely important phase and it is therefore of inestimable value to us that so much information on the subject is available.

*The small boats*    The Gokstad find also teaches us all we need to known about the small boats of the Viking Age. Here again we find the same high quality and well thought-out construction: basically the same as in the large ships, but with the deviations that naturally follow their smaller scale.

While the Gokstad find thus provides us with the most reliable information about the Viking ships and boats, it is the Oseberg find that teaches us most in all other respects, first and foremost on account of the large number of *wooden articles* found there. In

*Wooden articles*    the more "ordinary" Viking Age finds it is almost always only the metal objects that are preserved, but the Oseberg find gave us, for the first time, a clear picture of the important part played by wooden articles in every-day life: in farm work, in the kitchen and where other kinds of women's work was concerned, for example the making of textiles. All this was unknown before, and the finds have therefore given us a far fuller picture of the life and work of the people of that time, of their day-to-day surroundings and of the things that were of importance to them. They give us a good idea of how a Viking Age chieftain's hall was equipped—this was, in fact, by no means inferior to what historical sources tell about Norwegian castles of a much later date.

*Cultural relations*    The ship finds do not really give us any new information concerning cultural relations with foreign countries except, of course, that the ships are one of the prerequisites for such connections. However, they do provide a few new details that supplement the knowledge

74

gathered from other sources. The peacock in the Gokstad grave is one of these novelties, and the glass goblet in the Borre find is also the only one of its kind which we possess. Although the enamel work on the Buddha bucket is not without parallel in our collections, it is very rare.

Besides its importance to cultural history, the greatest significance of the Oseberg find is to the history of art, and here it is epoch-making in two fields: in textile history and in decorative wood-carving. In the field of textiles it is still too soon to assess the importance of the find, as the results of the research here have not yet been published. But the fact that a find contains fragments of textiles in such quantities is in itself of the greatest value, and when a large number of these prove to be fragments of tapestry it is clear that this material, too, is of major importance.

The same is the case with the wood-carving: here we had almost nothing before, and the small samples from Borre and Tune were not of much help. More was found at Gokstad, but even this was not significant enough to give any picture of the place of wood-carving in the history of our art. Then the Oseberg find with its treasures of wood-carving was discovered, and entirely new vistas were opened at once. Here, in the first place, is was shown that wood-carving could reach an unbelievably high technical standard, and it was also clear that it played a leading role from an artistic point of view. All our previous knowledge of art in Viking times was based on metal-work, but now it was found that this craft must almost be regarded as a minor one in comparison with the monumental wood-carving. It is clear, too, that is was the wood-carvers who were the leading, trend-setting artists of the period; the metal craftsmen followed them with their heavier material and small-scale work.

The wealth of wood-carving from the Oseberg find shows us a series of widely differing artistic personalities, who fortunately include among them one of the really great creative geniuses, "the Baroque Master", as Shetelig has called him. Two sleigh shafts and two animal head posts from his hand show us some salient features in one of the radical stylistic changes that took place in the Viking Age. An animal style with pure and elegant lines as its chief agent

75

had been inherited from the preceding epoch, the greatest stress being laid on the actual drawing, while the relief effect was of little importance. The decorative elements on the stem and stern of the ship show this style at the highest stage of its development, and we have the finest specimen of it in the "academic" animal head post.

But soon new tendencies began to appear in the wood-carving. The Viking expeditions brought in their wake a closer acquaintance with contemporary art in Europa, and one result of this was a wakening sense for greater plastic effect. This tendency emerges fully in the work of the "Baroque Master"; with him the new impulses are transformed into a new form of expression, the so-called "new Oseberg style", and this formed the basis for new developments, also in the next epoch.

It is quite unique that a single find should, in such a manner, throw light on one of the greatest changes in the history of art. It places the Oseberg find in quite a unique position among our archaeological finds, a stroke of luck that we can never hope to repeat even if anything as unlikely should happen as the discovery of yet another find of equal size and quality.

*The significance of the finds to national history* Finally we come to the most difficult, but perhaps the most intriguing of all the questions connected with the Viking ship finds, viz. whether the finds are directly connected with our national history. We must therefore try to combine archaeological fact with the few existing purely historical sources, first and foremost the Ynglingatal poem.

The nature of the problem is clear enough. We know that the unification of Norway into one kingdom began in Vestfold, and that the work of unification was completed in the second half of the ninth century. We have three ship graves in Vestfold from more or less the same period, and these are so richly furnished that they must be those of people of the very highest strata of society. The question is then, in the first place, whether these graves belong to members of the royal line, the Ynglinge line, and secondly whether, in that case, we can definitely determine which members of the royal line lay in each of the graves.

We cannot make any definite answer to these question, the evidence is not sufficiently reliable. But although the purely historical material

76

is so slight, we must nevertheless state that in *all probability* the northern branch of the Ynglinge line had their burial ground at Borre. Our Borre find may therefore be ascribed to a member of this royal line, and we must be entitled to assume that we also have the graves of several other members of the line on this site. There are still five large barrows and two great cairns here. The area is now a national park and a major tourist attraction. It is our most monumental burial ground from this period, and must originally have been even more impressive, for just over 100 years ago there were 9 large barrows here in addition to the two cairns.

*The barrows at Borre*

But if the barrows at Borre are connected with the Ynglinge line, then it is also quite likely that the same applies to the barrows at Oseberg and Gokstad, as these finds clearly originate from the same cultural environment as that of Borre. To the first part of our question we can therefore answer in the affirmative with a reasonable degree of certainty.

The second part of the question gives rise to greater difficulties: which members of the royal line lay in each of the graves? For the Borre find we must admit defeat, here we have nothing but the airiest theories. As for the Oseberg find, it has been maintained that this is the grave of Queen Aasa, the grandmother of Harald Fairhair, and that the Gokstad mound marks the burial place of her stepson, Olav Geirstadalv. Both of these theories are largely based on the interpretation of the names of the farms, which are both highly disputable. The attempted identification of the Gokstad chieftain was also partly founded on the first anatomical examination of the remains of the skeleton in the grave, but later research has shown this to be incorrect. The remains of the skeletons from Oseberg tend to *disprove* the theory of Queen Aasa, and strong criticism has been raised against it also for other reasons.

*Oseberg and Gokstad*

That the most remarkable woman in our oldest saga should also have provided us with our most remarkable archaeological discovery is naturally an attractive idea, but it is no more than a theory, and the basis on which it rests is certainly slight. When all is said and done it is really a matter of personal opinion, but this does not make the case any less interesting.

# BIBLIOGRAPHY

A considerable literature has been gradually built up around the Viking ship finds. The most important of the books will be mentioned here as a guide to those wishing to learn more about the finds.

The largest and most substantial work is the official publication "Osebergfunnet. Utgitt av Den norske stat" ("The Oseberg Find. Published by the Norwegian State") edited by A. W. Brøgger, Hj. Falk and Haakon Shetelig. Four volumes have been published to date (1917—1928), but the volume dealing with the textiles is still wanting. In the meantime, the most reliable information about this part of the find is to be found in Bjørn Hougens article "Oseberg-funnets billedvev" in the periodical "Viking" IV, Oslo, 1940.

The Gokstad find was published as early as 1882 by the man responsible for the excavation, N. Nicolaysen, in his book "Langskibet fra Gokstad ved Sandefjord" (The Viking Ship Discovered at Gokstad in Norway). The Tune ship was first described i Haakon Shetelig in "Tuneskibet" (Norske Oldfund, II, Kristiania 1917).

In this connection we would also mention A. W. Brøgger's thesis "Borrefundet og Vestfold-kongernes graver" Kristiania 1916. Although the ship from this find has not been preserved, it is nevertheless of great interest, not least on account of the significance of the actual site of the grave.

Many of the more specialized problems connected with the Viking ship finds have been dealt with in professional periodicals and other publications. Only a few treatises will be mentioned here, however. The first is "Vikingskipene. Deres forgjengere og etterfølgere" (The Viking Ships—their Ancestry and Evolution) by A. W. Brøgger & Haakon Shetelig, Oslo 1950, English edition 1953, which gives the best description of the actual ships, seen in a wider context. Then there are the articles by Fr. Johannessen "Osebergskibets stavner", Universitetets Oldsaksamlings Ärbok, 1928, and "Båtene fra Gokstadskipet", Viking IV, Oslo 1940; and finally Arne Emil Christensen, jr.: "Gokstadskipets stevner", Universitetets Oldsaksamlings Årbok, 1958—59, and "Færingen fra Gokstad", Viking XXIII, Oslo 1959.

The new Viking ship find from Klåstad in Tjølling has been provisionally published by the excavator, Arne Emil Christensen, jr. and Gunnar Leiro, Vestfoldminne 1976.

A more exhaustive account of the Viking ship finds from Skuldelev is given by Olaf Olsen and Ole Crumlin Pedersen in their joint work "The Skuldelev Ships" (II), (Acta Archaeologica, vol. XXXVIII, Copenhagen 1967).

# LIST OF ILLUSTRATIONS

Page

Sketch map of the sites .. .. .. .. .. .. .. .. .. .. .. .. .. 7

From the excavation of the Oseberg ship: the stern exposed .. .. .. .. 11

The Oseberg ship in the mound: the whole ship exposed .. .. .. .. .. 13

General arrangement of the Oseberg ship .. .. .. .. .. .. .. 16—17

The reconstructed Oseberg ship .. .. .. .. .. .. .. .. .. .. 19

The stern of the Oseberg ship, with the rudder .. .. .. .. .. .. .. 21

Piece of wood-carving from the Oseberg ship .. .. .. .. .. .. .. 23

The Oseberg cart .. .. .. .. .. .. .. .. .. .. .. .. .. 24

Wood-carving on the Oseberg cart, front end .. .. .. .. .. .. 26

Wood-carving on the Oseberg cart, left side .. .. .. .. .. .. .. 27

The largest of the sleighs in the Oseberg find, during the excavation .. .. 28

The largest of the sleighs in the Oseberg find, after restoration .. .. .. 29

Wood-carving on the Oseberg cart: stylized male head .. .. .. .. .. 31

Animal head from a sleigh in the Oseberg find .. .. .. .. .. .. .. 32

Animal head from a sleigh in the Oseberg find .. .. .. .. .. .. .. 33

The so-called «academic» animal head post from the Oseberg find .. .. .. 35

Detail from the carving on the «academic» animal head post .. .. .. .. 39

One of the smaller sleighs in the Oseberg find .. .. .. .. .. .. .. 41

Wood-carving on one of the sleighs in the Oseberg find .. .. .. .. .. 45

One of the «baroque» animal head posts in the Oseberg find .. .. .. .. 47

The «Buddha bucket» in the Oseberg find .. .. .. .. .. .. .. .. 48

Detail from the carving on one of the sleigh shafts in the Oseberg find .. .. 50

The Gokstad ship photographed during the excavation .. .. .. .. .. 55

The reconstructed Gokstad ship .. .. .. .. .. .. .. .. .. 57

Interior from the Gokstad ship .. .. .. .. .. .. .. .. .. .. 59

The Gokstad ship in the Viking Ship Hall .. .. .. .. .. .. .. .. 61

Interior of the Gokstad ship .. .. .. .. .. .. .. .. .. .. 62

The stern and rudder of the largest of the Gokstad boats .. .. .. .. .. 63

General arrangement of the Gokstad ship .. .. .. .. .. .. .. 64—65

Decorative carving from the Gokstad find .. .. .. .. .. .. .. .. 66

Reconstruction drawing of the Tune ship. Front view .. .. .. .. .. 70